Finding Your Purpose

A Guide to Personal Fulfillment

Revised Edition

Barbara J. Braham

A Crisp Fifty-Minute™ Series Book

This Fifty-Minute™ book is designed to be "read with a pencil." It is an excellent workbook for self-study as well as classroom learning. All material is copyright-protected and cannot be duplicated without permission from the publisher. *Therefore, be sure to order a copy for every training participant through our Web site, www.axzopress.com.*

Finding Your Purpose

A Guide to Personal Fulfillment

Revised Edition

Barbara J. Braham

CREDITS:
VP, Product Development: **Matt Gambino**
Editor: **Ann Gosch**
Production Editor: **Genevieve McDermott**
Production Artists: **Nicole Phillips and Betty Hopkins**

Trademarks
Crisp Fifty-Minute Series is a trademark of Axzo Press.

Some of the product names and company names used in this book have been used for identification purposes only and may be trademarks or registered trademarks of their respective manufacturers and sellers.

Disclaimer
We reserve the right to revise this publication and make changes from time to time in its content without notice.

ISBN 10: 1-56052-684-X
ISBN 13: 978-1-56052-684-1
Library of Congress Catalog Card Number 2003100054
Printed in the United States of America

6 7 8 9 09 08

Learning Objectives For:

FINDING YOUR PURPOSE

The objectives for *Finding Your Purpose, Revised Edition* are listed below. They have been developed to guide the user to the core issues covered in this book.

THE OBJECTIVES OF THIS BOOK ARE TO HELP THE USER:

1) Discover his or her life purpose

2) Explore barriers that can get in the way of defining life purpose

3) Gain tools for overcoming these barriers for a more fulfilling life

ASSESSING PROGRESS

A Crisp Series **assessment** is available for this book. The 25-item, multiple-choice and true/false questionnaire allows the reader to evaluate his or her comprehension of the subject matter.

To download the assessment and answer key, go to www.axzopress.com and search on the book title.

Assessments should not be used in any employee selection process.

About the Author

Barbara J. Braham, MSW, MCC, is a business coach, speaker, facilitator, and author. She has delivered hundreds of seminars to organizations across the country since 1985. Her topics include "Manager as Coach," "Finding Your Purpose," and "Living a Legacy Moment to Moment."

Formerly associate director of a multi-million dollar mental health center, she facilitates strategic planning retreats and coaches leaders who want to move their organizations forward. She is the author of 11 books and two audiocassette programs. She has served as president of the Ohio chapter of the National Speakers Association and of the Central Ohio Chapter of the International Coach Federation.

For information about her coaching or seminars, visit her Web site www.bbraham.com, or e-mail her at barbara@bbraham.com.

Acknowledgments

Special thanks to:

John Travis—for what he's taught me about the Dharma

My Florida Circle—Linda Bailey, Sandy Campbell, Ph.D., Becky Nickol, Wendy Warman—for years of thought-provoking dialogue

Margaret Lewis and Nancy Pettigrew—for showing me how we dream our purpose and it dreams us

The BATS—Leslie Charles, Mary Jane Mapes, Marilynn Semonick—for sharing the journey of living on purpose

Jane and Granville Braham—for their love and support

The people at Crisp—Mary Kay Beeby, Mike Crisp, Diana West, and Debbie Woodbury—who've supported this book over the years

Rick Braveheart—for being my most cherished thinking partner and the greatest blessing in my life

Preface

WARNING!

The book you are about to read could change your life. You will ask yourself many questions as you go through life, but none are more basic, more fundamental, more critical than "Why am I here?" and "What is my purpose?" To answer these questions is to face the mystery of your life. If you are willing to take this risk, this book is for you!

When you ask yourself "What is my purpose?" you embark upon a journey of personal and spiritual growth. It is a rewarding and difficult journey. In this book you will be asked tough questions. If you are to benefit fully from this book, you will need an inquisitive spirit, an open heart, and the commitment to complete each of the exercises honestly—beginning with the one on page viii.

If you take seriously the process outlined, you will discover insights that can lead to significant life changes. People have been known to quit their jobs and change careers after completing these exercises. Some have moved to other parts of the country. Still others have married or divorced. Without a doubt, engaging this question in a deep way leads to a more fulfilling life.

In this revised edition, you will have an opportunity to put "What is my purpose?" into the context of where you are in the life cycle. As my own life has evolved, I have discovered that the meaning we attach to this question changes with each decade of life experience. You will have the opportunity to find out what "the question behind the question" is for you.

Finding Your Purpose is both easy to read and extremely challenging. You can skim through the pages in about an hour; the exercises take you through your lifetime. If you are willing to face yourself at this intimate level, read on! You will not be disappointed with whom you discover yourself to be.

Barbara J. Braham

Contents

Part 1: What Is Purpose?

Living "On Purpose" 3

What Other Authors Say About Purpose 4

Making Distinctions 5

Exploring the Role of Passion 8

Distinguishing Purpose from Meaning 10

Expressing Your Purpose in All Your Life Domains 14

Seeking Purpose Through the Life Cycle 17

Unveiling Your Purpose 20

Part 2: Veil #1: Busyness

Does Busyness Equal Success? 23

Taking Time for What You Enjoy 26

Recognizing Your Talents 31

Identifying Your Skills 34

Merging Your Talents and Skills 37

Removing the Veil of Busyness 39

Cultivating Silence 40

Part 3: Veil #2: What Will Other People Think?

The Tyranny of the Shoulds 45

Understanding the Three Layers of Shoulds 47

Removing the Veil: Clarify Your Values 49

Replacing Shoulds with Values Statements 55

Resolving Values Conflicts 56

Listening to Your Intuition 58

Letting Go of Blocks to Intuition 59

Amplifying Your Intuition 62

Part 4: Veil #3: I'm Not _____ Enough

Rethinking Your Perceived Shortcomings 67

Avoiding the Comparison Trap 68

Removing the Veil: Raising Your Self-Esteem 69

Analyzing Your Self-Talk 71

Giving Yourself Daily Acknowledgments 72

Keeping a Gratitude Journal 74

Replacing Negative Self-Talk with Affirmations 75

Discovering Your Uniqueness 78

Part 5: Veil #4: Fear

Understanding the Veil of Fear 83

Interpreting Fear as a Step Toward Growth 85

Recognizing Your Sense of Fear 86

Befriending Your Fears 89

Removing the Veil: Taking Risks 92

Getting Started with Smaller Risks 94

Taking Steps to Improve Your Risk Taking 96

Part 6: Veil #5: The Seduction of More

Rethinking the Quest for "More" 99

Examining the "Have, Do, Be" Formula for Happiness 101

Removing the Veil: Shifting to *Being* 102

Deepening Your Understanding of *Being* 103

Reaching a Conclusion About Your Purpose 105

Final Word 107

Additional Reading 108

Your Journey Starts Here

Are you wondering what your purpose is? Read through the following statements and check those that are true for you. These will give you insight about the areas you may want to focus on as you work through *Finding Your Purpose*.

- ❏ I sometimes feel that there is something missing in my life.
- ❏ I don't feel much joy in my life.
- ❏ I don't like what I'm doing for a living, but I don't know what else to do.
- ❏ There is something I have always longed to do, but I can't find the courage to do it.
- ❏ I believe I could contribute more than I do.
- ❏ It seems like I spend my life doing what I "should" do instead of doing what I feel called to do.
- ❏ I don't ever seem to have any time for myself; I'm always busy.
- ☑ I'm successful, but there is an empty feeling to the success; I don't feel fulfilled.
- ❏ I have all the things that are supposed to make me happy, except I'm not happy.
- ☑ I'm easily influenced by what other people think I should do.
- ☑ I wonder if being successful is worth the price I'm paying.
- ☑ It is hard for me to relax; I feel that I need to be doing something all the time.
- ❏ I think about the questions: Why am I here? Do I have a purpose? What is my destiny?
- ❏ I believe that there has to be more to life than what I have been experiencing.
- ☑ I'm in transition and I don't know what is next.
- ❏ I am reassessing my spiritual beliefs.
- ❏ I feel that there is something I am "supposed" to be doing, but I'm not sure what it is.
- ☑ I want to make a difference in the world.

What Is Purpose?

"We shall not cease from exploration, and the end of all our exploring will be to arrive where we started and know the place for the first time."

—T. S. Eliot

Living "On Purpose"

Every once in a while you meet people whose work is inspired. They exude enthusiasm. They appear to genuinely care about what they are doing, the people with whom they work, and the people they serve. They express a joy that seems to come from deep within; it is not forced or superficial. You sense their genuineness and authenticity, and you do not believe they are playing a role.

When you meet such people you realize that their work is consistent with their purpose. You might say they are working "on purpose." The word *work*, in this context, is used in the broadest sense, not in the narrowest sense of paid employment. In his book, *The Reinvention of Work*, author Matthew Fox says it well when he writes:

> *We must learn to speak of the difference between a job and work. We may be forced to take a job serving food at a fast-food place for [minimum wage] in order to pay our bills, but work is something else. Work comes from inside out; work is the expression of our soul, our inner being. It is unique to the individual; it is creative. Work is an expression of the Spirit at work in the world through us.*

People Who Love What They Do

Take a minute now and think of people in your life who seem to love what they do. Write down the names (or jobs, if you do not know the names) of three of these people. Then describe what there is about them that makes you think they know and live their purpose.

Person #1: _____

_____

_____

Person #2: _____

_____

_____

Person #3: _____

_____

_____

What Other Authors Say About Purpose

Many authors have written on the subject of purpose, especially in the past few decades as more people have pursued spiritual growth. Each author brings a unique voice to this common subject. As you read through these quotes, put a check in the box next to the ones that speak loudest to you. What is it about the quote that touches, inspires, or affirms you?

☑ Vocation is the place where your deep gladness and the world's hunger meets.

> —Frederick Buechner, *Wishful Thinking: A Seeker's ABC*

❑ ... to feel that what we do is right for ourselves and good for the world at exactly the same time is one of the great triumphs of human existence.

> —David Whyte, *Crossing the Unknown Sea*

❑ The "midlife" crisis with which the psychotherapists grappled probably reflects the fact that at midlife, one's own death becomes less theoretical and more probable. Goals of money, security, fame, sex, or power might formerly have given purpose to life. With experience, the limited nature of such satisfactions becomes increasingly evident ... the search for meaning becomes increasingly urgent.

> —Arthur J. Deikman, *The Observing Self*

❑ But each incarnation, you might say, has a potentiality, and the mission of life is to live that potentiality. How do you do it? My answer is, "Follow your bliss." There is something inside you that knows when you are in the center, that knows when you are on the beam or off the beam. And if you get off the beam to earn money, you have lost your life. And if you stay in the center and don't get any money, you still have your bliss.

> —Joseph Campbell, *The Power of Myth*

❑ The historic period in which we live is a period of reawakening to a commitment to higher values, a reawakening of individual purpose, and reawakening of the longing to fulfill that purpose in life.

> —Robert Fritz, *The Path of Least Resistance*

❑ My advice is to live your life—allow that wonderful inner intelligence to speak through you... Don't climb the ladder of success only to find it is leaning against the wrong wall.

> —Bernie Siegel, M.D., *Love, Medicine and Miracles*

Making Distinctions

Mission, vision, vocation, calling, destiny, bliss, passion, meaning. These are just some of the words that have been used to describe our human need to identify and express our purpose. But are these words all really talking about the same thing?

A mission statement is common in a business. Your company probably has one. It describes what the company does. You might have a personal mission statement. It would describe what you do. For example, your mission might be to design systems that save time and money. But that is not your life's purpose. Purpose is bigger than that.

A vision statement also is often found in businesses. A vision is a picture of a future you would like to create. You might create a vision statement for yourself. In the Native American tradition, a person goes on a vision quest to discover his or her personal vision. Some people create a vision map, which is a collage of pictures that represents the future they want to create. An example of a personal vision statement is "to own my own company." Vision statements, like purpose statements, can be very big. You could have a vision of world peace. This is still not your life purpose. Your life purpose lies behind your vision and breathes life into it. If your vision is world peace, then your purpose might be "to be a voice for peace."

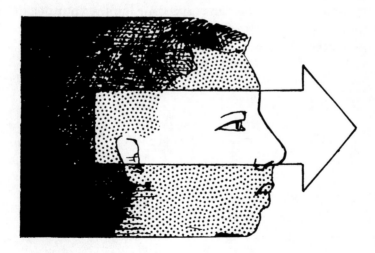

Vision and Goals in Relation to Purpose

When people have a vision, it often leads them to set long-term goals. Perhaps your vision is to be a leader in your company. It may take you 20 years to develop the skills and acquire the knowledge that will allow you to step into a senior management position. When you achieve this, you may be surprised to find that an emptiness follows. That is because you mistook a long-term goal and vision for your purpose. When the goal is achieved, there isn't anything to take its place and you can feel as if you have lost your purpose. You have not lost your purpose. You need to find it.

Many people in their 30s and 40s believe they are living on purpose when in fact they are pursuing long-term goals. The achievement of the goals and subsequent feelings of emptiness can lead to a time of introspection and questioning. That may be why you are reading this book right now.

Purpose answers the existential question *why:* Why are you here, on this planet, at this time? Are you here to do something? Are you here to be someone? Is there a difference in those two questions?

When you find an answer to the *why* question, the answer will hold up in every part of your life. It will apply to your family life, your work life, your social life, your community life. If you have not found an answer that fits in every domain of your life, you have not found the answer yet.

For example, your purpose might be "to serve others." This is a very simple and profound purpose statement. You can serve your family, your neighbors, your co-workers, customers, and also strangers you meet in the grocery store. You can be on purpose no matter where you are or what you do.

LABEL THE STATEMENT

Below is a list of statements. Some of them are purpose statements, some are mission statements, some are goals, and some are vision statements. Read each statement and decide for yourself which one it is. Write your answer in the space provided.

1. My _____ is to raise my children to be healthy, productive adults.

2. My _____ is to compete in the Olympics.

3. My _____ is to be kind.

4. My _____ is to use my creativity to design Web pages.

5. My _____ is to express my creativity.

6. My _____ is to teach.

7. My _____ is to be a voice for sustainability.

8. My _____ is to write a best-selling book.

9. My _____ is to help customers solve their problems.

10. My _____ is to use color, texture, and design to create comfortable living and work spaces.

Author's suggested answers: 1. mission or goal; 2. goal or vision; 3. purpose; 4. mission; 5. purpose; 6. purpose; 7. purpose; 8. vision or goal; 9. mission or goal; 10. mission

Exploring the Role of Passion

Vocation, calling, destiny, and bliss are words that point toward the same thing—purpose. Throughout this book you will see the word *passion* used to refer to purpose. There are several reasons for choosing this word. First, look at the word carefully. You will see that it contains the essence of what purpose is about:

pass - i - on

Isn't that what you want to do—to make a difference in the lives of others and leave something of yourself behind—pass yourself (i) on? None of us wants to think that we have lived and died without leaving any trace of our uniqueness behind. We want to believe that we have made a contribution in the world. Leaving a legacy is another way of saying that you have lived a life of purpose.

Notice that the *i* in "pass-i-on" is lowercase and not uppercase. That is intentional. A capital *I* would suggest that purpose were in some way about ego. It is not. Remember, purpose is a spiritual question that we live out in the material world. What is most important is the difference or contribution that one makes, not the *I* who made the difference or contribution.

Tapping in to Your Feelings

Another reason we use the word *passion* when referring to purpose is that both terms are about feeling. To fulfill a passion is to express deeply held feelings. Passion is not intellectual or rational. It comes from the heart—it is a calling. You do not *think* about what your purpose is, you *feel* or *know* your purpose. You do not figure it out; you experience it. Finding your purpose is less analytical and more intuitive.

Passion implies desire; and your passion, if given a voice, will arouse you to take action. Once known, it demands to be fulfilled. If we fail to listen, we suffer stress, fatigue, frustration, or dissatisfaction. You may be feeling dissatisfied in your present work because you feel no passion for what you do.

Passion is compelling; it creates an inner sense of urgency quite distinct from the external events of our lives. Passion allows us to be truly alive!

Now that you have (1) thought about people you know who are working on purpose, (2) read the quotes of others about purpose, and (3) considered the distinctions between purpose, mission, vision, and goals, it is your turn to reflect on your own ideas about purpose. What words or phrases would you use to describe it?

To me, the definition of purpose is:

_____

_____

Distinguishing Purpose from Meaning

Is there a difference between purpose and meaning? Yes, there is an important distinction. You can have a meaningful life whether or not you believe you have a purpose, whether or not you have uncovered your purpose. Meaning is the significance you attach to an event, person, or situation. You can have meaningful work, no matter what you do, if you decide to assign it meaning. To give something meaning is a rational, left-brain act. A well-known story makes this distinction clear.

Two stone masons were at work when a visitor came upon them. Curious, the visitor asked the first one what he was doing. He replied that he was cutting stone. Then the visitor moved on to the second stone mason and asked the same question. His reply was, "I'm building a cathedral." The second man had given his work meaning.

Assigning Meaning to Life Events

To a large extent the meaning you ascribe to events determines the quality of your life. You have no doubt heard the expressions, "things happen for a reason" and "there are no accidents in life." If you subscribe to either of these statements, then you are in the meaning-making business. If you get laid off from your job, you can decide that it happened because there is something better waiting for you. You can decide that this is a blessing in disguise because you had been working too many hours and your health was suffering.

You can just as easily take being laid off as proof that you are being treated unfairly. You can decide it means you will never get ahead. There is no right or wrong to meaning-making. As human beings we all do it. But there is an emotional charge to meaning-making. We feel good when we give a situation positive meaning (there is a better job waiting). We feel bad when we give a situation negative meaning (I am being treated unfairly).

Are you making meaning in a way that serves you? In other words, are you interpreting situations in a way that inspires and uplifts you? Or does your meaning-making lead you to feel discouraged and down?

Choose three recent events and briefly jot them down in the first column. In the second column, describe what meaning you have assigned to these events. What kind of meaning-maker are you?

Events That Are Meaningful to Me

Events:	What They Mean to Me:
_____	_____
_____	_____
_____	_____
_____	_____
_____	_____
_____	_____
_____	_____

Accepting Life as It Comes

You do have an alternative to meaning-making. That alternative is called *acceptance;* or in some spiritual traditions, the word *surrender* is used. You can accept life as it presents itself to you. You can simply be with whatever is happening (although it takes considerable discipline and practice) without judging it positive or negative, good or bad. Acceptance is not passive. It is an active process that may require action from you. It takes someone with an advanced spiritual practice to accept life as it is, moment to moment, without adding interpretation.

As a practice, try noticing yourself as a meaning-maker. Before you settle on an interpretation of a situation, ask yourself these questions:

> ➤ What other ways could I assign meaning to this?

> ➤ Is the meaning that I am giving to this situation serving me?

> ➤ What if, instead of assigning meaning to this, I simply accepted it as the way life is right now?

Purpose is quite different from meaning. You do not *bestow* purpose as you bestow meaning. Purpose flows from deep within you. An emotional charge of pleasant or unpleasant does not accompany purpose as it does meaning.

Purpose is connected to the potential that you hold as a human being, much as the acorn holds the potential for an oak tree. It will sustain you throughout all the changes and phases of your life. It is the center that holds. Purpose is what you are called to do. It is a part of your uniqueness. Living on purpose is one way to live a meaningful life.

WRITE YOUR PURPOSE—FIRST DRAFT

You may be thinking very differently about what purpose is and is not, now that you have read this far in the book. Before you read further, write what you believe your purpose is. It is okay if it is vague at this point. It will become clearer as you work through this book.

My purpose is:

_____

_____

_____

_____

_____

_____

_____

_____

_____

_____

_____

_____

_____

_____

_____

_____

_____

_____

_____

_____

_____

Expressing Your Purpose in All Your Life Domains

It is easy to think of purpose in relation to work and home. But these are only two of eight *domains,* or areas, of your life. And your purpose will flow through every part of your life. If your purpose shows up in only one domain, then you may have a goal, mission, or a vision but not your purpose.

The Eight Domains of Life

➤ Work/Career (including volunteer work)

➤ Physical (your body)

➤ Financial (spend, save, donate money)

➤ Leisure (play, hobbies, travel)

➤ Family (immediate, extended, and "created")

➤ Spiritual (prayer, meditation, spiritual practices)

➤ Creative (writing, cooking, gardening, painting, crafting, etc.)

➤ Learning (reading, classes, e-learning, experiential, study groups)

Think of these eight domains as pieces of a pie. Each piece fits into the pie that is your life, as represented by the pie chart that follows.

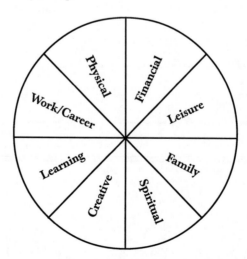

Learning by Example

To see how your purpose might flow through all eight domains, let's say your purpose is "to express creativity." Then you might express your purpose in each domain as follows:

➤ At work, you might be a creative problem solver, and you may have chosen a creative profession such as graphic design.

➤ In the physical domain you could be creative in getting exercise, regularly varying sports and weight-training routines.

➤ Financially, you might have designed a creative system for tracking your expenses.

➤ Your leisure and creative domains could overlap as you pursue creative pastimes such as woodworking or beading, playing a musical instrument, or acting in community theater.

➤ In your family you might bring creativity to celebrating holidays, telling bedtime stories, and performing everyday tasks.

➤ In your spiritual life you could focus your creativity on daily practices to enrich yourself and others.

➤ In the learning domain, your creativity might show up in ways to make learning fun.

It is easy to confuse the expression of purpose in one domain of your life for your purpose. For example, imagine that work is the largest slice of your life pie, and the other seven domains are only slivers of the pie. In that situation you might think that being a graphic designer is your purpose. But unless your statement of purpose flows through every domain, you don't yet have a purpose statement.

This doesn't mean that you are necessarily living your purpose in every domain at this moment. For instance, you might not be in a position at this time to apply your creativity to your family life. Or you may not be involved in any kind of exercise program for your physical domain. The point is that your purpose could be expressed in each domain, whether or not it actually is right now.

Most people find that as they move through life, they live their purpose in more and more domains. When you are expressing your purpose in all the domains, you can say you are "living on purpose."

TEST YOUR PURPOSE STATEMENT

Now it is your turn. Take the purpose statement you drafted on page 13 and see if it flows across all of the domains. You may not be living it yet in all the domains; that is okay. Remember, your purpose and its expression will evolve over time and you may not be ready yet to express it in all areas of your life. You want to test your statement to see if it is big enough to qualify as a purpose statement.

My purpose statement:

_____

_____

How it is or might be expressed in the following domains:

Work/Career: _____

_____

Physical: _____

_____

Financial: _____

_____

Leisure: _____

_____

Family: _____

_____

Spiritual: _____

_____

Creative: _____

_____

Learning: _____

_____

Seeking Purpose Through the Life Cycle

From the time you are born until the time you die, you are growing and changing. As you go through life, you need to complete specific developmental tasks before you move on to the next stage. You are no doubt familiar with the developmental tasks of childhood and adolescence. When you reach adulthood, it is easy to think you are through with these tasks. Of course you recognize that there will be changes: marriage, children, career moves, empty nest, aging parents, retirement, and so on. But you may not have related these external events to your internal emotional, psychological, and spiritual growth.

The question "What is my purpose?" means different things depending upon where you are in your life cycle. If you are in your 20s, this question is often about what job to take, what course of study to pursue, if to marry or not, if to have a family or not.

When you reach your 30s, the question does not go away. But what is behind it changes. By this time you have had a job or two or three. "What is my purpose?" is no longer about finding a job. Now it is about finding a career that might sustain you, a career that uses your talents and skills, yet aligns with your values, which are becoming increasingly clearer.

The Midlife Transition

From the late 30s through the late 40s you make the great midlife transition. For some people this is a time of crisis as they reluctantly let go of the first half of life, while having no clear picture of the second half. The key issues that accompany this transition are accepting loss, completing your past, integrating your shadow, and realizing spiritual awakening or wholeness. The loss of a job or a relationship can trigger the question, "What is my purpose?" Completing the past may mean coming to terms with the fact that you chose work that pleased your family, but not yourself. Integrating your shadow can mean discovering the talents and gifts you possess that you have not used until now.

And finally, the search for your purpose is one entry point to spiritual awakening or wholeness.

The psychiatrist Carl Jung was one of the first people to write about midlife and spirituality. He said, "Among all my patients in the second half of life—that is to say, over 35—there has not been one whose problem in the last resort was not that of finding a religious outlook on life ... This of course has nothing to do with a particular creed or membership in a church."

The midlife transition is the developmental stage during which "What is my purpose?" means coming to terms with the meaning of your life. You want to know that your work is making a difference. Now the questions behind the question are much deeper and might include:

➤ Who am I?

➤ How can I make a contribution in the world?

➤ Why am I here?

These questions are critical if you want to continue to grow toward self-actualization. And the questions are uncomfortable. Do you know people who have had an affair, bought a sports car, or found some other way to distract themselves from these questions? If you are in the time of midlife transition, are you avoiding these questions?

Purpose and Legacy in the Later Years

Once you are firmly planted in the second half of life, the meaning behind the question, "What is my purpose?" shifts yet again. Now your focus is on living your life in alignment with your purpose in a deep and nourishing way. The expectations of the outer culture have less impact on you. You are increasingly able to live your life from the inside out. The confidence that comes with clarity about why you are here allows you to live with more authenticity as you say no to things that are not aligned with your purpose and yes to things that are. This is the time in life when you have the possibility of shaping the world through the power of living your life on purpose.

For people in their 60s and beyond, the question becomes, "Am I leaving a legacy by living out my purpose?" Now the wish is to be remembered as the authentic expression of your purpose.

Wherever you are in your life cycle, "What is Your Purpose?" is important. Your purpose will not change from week to week, or even year to year. That is what goals do. But it will evolve over decades of your life if you enter the question deeply. This is a book that you can come back to again and again as "What is my purpose?" changes from being a question about a job, to a question of career, to a question of contribution, to a question of an aligned life, to a question about legacy.

Unveiling Your Purpose

The assumption throughout this book is that you *have* a purpose. But if you are still unclear about your purpose, it may be because it is hidden from view by one or more of following five veils:

Veil #1: *Busyness*

Veil #2: *What Will Other People Think?*

Veil #3: *I'm Not _____ Enough*

Veil #4: *Fear*

Veil #5: *The Seduction of More*

Any of these veils may be between you and knowing your purpose. If you can remove these veils, your purpose will become clear to you.

The remainder of this book will look in detail at the five veils. After each veil is described, you will be offered one or more tools you can use to remove that veil.

PART 2

Veil #1: Busyness

> *The challenge to find meaning in what you do is at the core of the new work ethic. Employees want more than just a paycheck from their work. They want to feel connected to their organization's mission and vision. They look toward the organization as a place where they can grow and accomplish their own personal vision as well as the organization's larger purpose."*
>
> **—Cynthia Scott and Dennis Jaffe,** *Take This Job and Love It*

22

Does Busyness Equal Success?

Our society often equates success with busyness. In some circles, the more hours you can say you work, the more you are respected. That is the opposite of how it has been throughout recorded history. In the past, a sign of success was the ability to have time that was not committed. Having leisure time—the time to contemplate the world and the time to ask questions such as "Why am I here?"—was considered a sign of success. But not today.

To equate success with busyness has created problems. After trying to accomplish more, we are suffering the consequences: increased stress, illness, alienation from loved ones, and an overwhelming feeling of time poverty. These are symptoms of a life that is out of balance.

Look at the word busyness. Just one small change—from *y* to *i*—and you have a significant cause of the problem: business...work. Constant activity alienates you from yourself. You become too busy to know who you are or what you stand for. You have trouble setting priorities because you do not take time to clarify your values.

Less Is More

Finding your purpose requires you to slow down and create enough space in your life that your purpose can emerge and reveal itself to you. In their book, *Cultural Creatives: How 50 Million People are Changing the World,* Paul Ray and Sherry Ruth Anderson describe a quiet movement of people committed to voluntary simplicity, living in greater harmony with the rhythms of nature, and finding and living a life of purpose. You might be one of them.

Paradoxes have been sprinkled throughout this book to help you see that finding your purpose is not an either/or proposition. Your purpose emerges and you create it. The first paradox below addresses the concept that if you think there is something missing in your life, doing more will not help you find what it is. Increasing the activity in your life will only solidify the veil of busyness.

PARADOX: *Less is more*

How Busy Are You?

Take a few minutes to think about your own level of busyness and your attitudes about it. Write your answers in the spaces provided.

1. How many hours do you work in the average week?

   _____

2. List the outside commitments you have. Include professional, social, and community commitments.

   _____

   _____

3. When did you work during a scheduled family activity in the past month? For example, did you work on a day when your child was playing in a soccer game?

   _____

   _____

4. When was the last time you had an hour alone with no demands?

   _____

   _____

5. Do you have all the latest timesaving devices? For example, do you have a cell phone, a pager, a handheld computer, a Palm Pilot or other PDA?

   _____

   _____

6. Do you ever feel things are happening too quickly?

   _____

   _____

7. Do you feel guilty if you are not doing something?

   _____

   _____

CONTINUED

=CONTINUED=

8. Do you pride yourself on your ability to multitask?

_____

_____

9. Are you sleep-deprived?

_____

_____

10. Are you expected or do you try to be available 24/7?

_____

_____

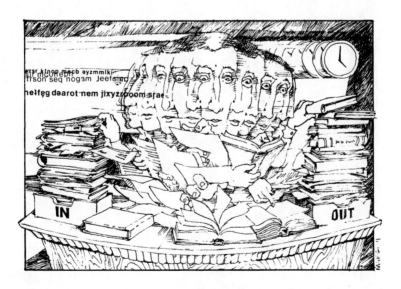

Taking Time for What You Enjoy

In a life run by busyness, you may sacrifice what you enjoy for what is exciting. Enjoyment and excitement are not the same. Excitement is a stimulant and can be experienced fast. Excitement also has an addictive quality to it. Unfortunately, it is an addiction that gets harder and harder to satisfy. Think about what it takes today for a movie to be "exciting" compared with just a decade ago.

Enjoyment is deeper and more abiding than excitement. Enjoyment takes time. It is something you savor. When you are living on purpose, you will notice that you enjoy most of your life. You also will notice that the highs and lows even out as you trade the rush of excitement for the satisfaction of enjoyment.

Because of busyness, you may not take time to do the things you enjoy. It is easy to fall into automatically doing what has to be done, what you committed your-self to last week or last month. A steady diet of this and you begin to lose touch with the things that bring you pleasure and joy. Life can come to feel like a lot of "have-tos" instead of "want-tos." In fact, you may even forget what you enjoy! If this is true for you, it will be harder for you to identify your passion.

If you are in the midlife transition, you may discover that you no longer enjoy what you used to enjoy. You may need to slow down to discover what you enjoy in your new stage of life. You will need to experiment and try new things.

WHAT DO YOU ENJOY?

Listed below are the eight domains of life. In the spaces that follow each one, list two things you currently enjoy, two things you used to enjoy, and two things you might enjoy.

Work/Career

Enjoy:

_____

_____

Used to enjoy:

_____

_____

Might enjoy:

_____

_____

Physical

Enjoy:

_____

_____

Used to enjoy:

_____

_____

Might enjoy:

_____

_____

CONTINUED

Financial

Enjoy:

_____

_____

Used to enjoy:

_____

_____

Might enjoy:

_____

_____

Leisure

Enjoy:

_____

_____

Used to enjoy:

_____

_____

Might enjoy:

_____

_____

Family

Enjoy:

_____

_____

CONTINUED

Used to enjoy:

_____

_____

Might enjoy:

_____

_____

Spiritual

Enjoy:

_____

_____

Used to enjoy:

_____

_____

Might enjoy:

_____

_____

Creative

Enjoy:

_____

_____

Used to enjoy:

_____

_____

CONTINUED

Might enjoy:

_____

_____

Learning

Enjoy:

_____

_____

Used to enjoy:

_____

_____

Might enjoy:

_____

_____

Looking at how you have completed this exercise, what does it suggest to you? Are there things you enjoy and are not doing? Do you need to make time for these things? Are you still doing things that you do not enjoy doing anymore? Do you need to stop doing them? Are there new things you need to try? What one new thing will you try this week?

Recognizing Your Talents

We each come into this world blessed with specific talents or gifts. These are abilities we have that seem to come naturally. These gifts can be a clue to our purpose in that they can help us fulfill whatever it is we believe we are here to do. Some examples are athletic ability, dexterity, musical talent, taste, artistic ability, sense of humor, ease with people, comfort with numbers, and so on.

Take time now to think about your talents. This is part of what makes you unique as a person. List at least five talents before you go on.

My talents include:

1. _____
2. _____
3. _____
4. _____
5. _____

Did you have trouble with this exercise? Many people cannot identify five talents. They may never have taken the time to think about their talents, or they may not want to brag or boast. Don't worry! To acknowledge and own your talents will not send you on an ego trip. Quite the contrary: Without this basic self-awareness, you cannot make much of an impact on the world.

You may minimize or ignore your talents because they come easily to you. You may assume that if it is easy for you, it is easy for everyone. This is a way you diminish yourself and veil your passion. If something comes easily to you, do not assume that it is easy for everyone. Instead, use that as a clue that it is one of your talents.

HOW DO OTHERS SEE YOUR TALENTS?

If you could not write down at least five talents, here is your next assignment. (You may want to do this even if you did identify five talents, because it is so rewarding and affirming.) Think of five people who know you well. These could be friends, family members, neighbors, or colleagues. Arrange a time when you can speak with them alone, without being interrupted, and ask them these questions:

➤ What do you think makes me special?

➤ What is there about me that is unique?

➤ What are my talents?

Then listen and write down the answers they give you. When you have interviewed five people, look over all your notes and make a composite list. Write down the comments that were similar. Do the talents you listed match what others said?

Name _____

_____

_____

Name _____

_____

_____

Name _____

_____

_____

Name _____

_____

_____

CONTINUED

=CONTINUED=

Name _____

_____

_____

My composite list of talents:

_____

_____

Identifying Your Skills

Now that you have had a chance to think about your talents, let's take a look at your skills. A *skill* is something you have learned to do. What competencies do you have as a result of training, experience, or education? Some examples include using computers, fixing an automobile, organizing, being assertive, operating equipment, and managing time. Most people have dozens of skills that immediately come to mind. The list that follows may trigger other skills of yours that you have forgotten about.

You may discover that the skills list includes some of the traits you listed as your talents in the preceding exercises. That is because people often work to develop skills in areas where they do not have talents. For example, some people have a talent for organization. It is a gift and seems to come naturally to them. But others work hard to learn how to organize through taking seminars, reading books, or training on the job—and eventually become skilled at organizing. You will need to make a judgment call about whether the traits you possess qualify as *skills* or *talents*.

Skills by Category

This is not intended as an all-inclusive list of skills. It is designed to remind you of roles you play in your life and the skills you might use in these various roles.

Domestic

Cooking

Cleaning

Budgeting

Shopping

Gardening

Decorating

Repairing

Raising children

Entertaining

Carpentry

_____

Business

Leadership

Planning

Managing

Delegating

Computing

Coaching

Writing

Accounting/Working

with numbers

Giving presentations

_____

Recreational

Golfing

Soccer

Hiking

Reading

Music

Biking

Painting

Crafts

Surfing the Web

_____

Interpersonal

Listening

Assertiveness

Asking questions

Motivating

Selling

Persuading

Establishing rapport

Negotiating

Problem solving

_____

Self-Management

Relaxing

Positive thinking

Emotional intelligence

Imagination

Visualizing

Following through

Initiating

Risk taking

Learning

_____

List Your Own Skills

First write down the skills that immediately come to mind for you. Then augment this list with others you picked up from the preceding skills list.

_____

_____

_____

_____

_____

_____

_____

Merging Your Talents and Skills

Is there any relationship between your talents and your skills? Have you developed skills that build on your gifts? For example, you may have natural athletic abilities, but have you developed any specific skills such as tennis? Or maybe you have a gift for writing. Have you developed skills in your use of language? Perhaps you have a natural eye for colors that go together. Have you developed any skills in interior design or wardrobe planning? You can make maximum use of your talents by developing skills around them.

Your unique blend of talents and skills is a clue to your purpose. Your talents and skills will help you fulfill your purpose.

In the chart below, record your talents and the skills you have developed around each talent.

Talent	Skills I Developed Around This Talent

Skills That Use Your Talents

Remember the parable of the talents? Do not bury your talents, but instead cultivate them. This may mean you need to develop some skills to take your talents into the world. The more you use your talents, the more you will discover that life flows easily.

People are beginning to see that it is wiser to focus on developing your talents than it is to try to develop your weaknesses. In their book, *Now, Discover Your Strengths,* authors Marcus Buckingham and Donald Clifton point out that the most successful people, and the most productive businesses, focus on how to identify and leverage strengths. With a strength assessment tool included, it is a good book to read if you are still struggling with recognizing your talents.

Removing the Veil of Busyness

If busyness is preventing you from knowing your passion, what can you do about it? You can allocate time for silence and solitude. Rather than complaining about how busy you are and how you do not have time to do the things you want to do, focus your energies on creating time for yourself.

Creative geniuses have always required and cherished significant time alone. Creativity cannot emerge when your mind is cluttered with business and busyness. Your greatest thoughts and ideas will come in times of quiet reflection and stillness. This is a key to uncovering your passion. Remember, your purpose is not something you can think through and figure out. Instead, it is something that you feel, experience, intuit. It comes from deep inside of you.

Imagine yourself trying to talk on the telephone while a jet flies overhead, a rock band plays at a party in the next room, and a child cries next to you. It would be difficult, wouldn't it? And so it is with hearing your purpose. Your life may be so busy that it drowns out your inner voice. You do not need to make your inner voice louder; it is already perfectly clear. You need to turn down the volume in your life so you can listen to your inner voice.

Cultivating Silence

> *Silence stands outside the world of profit and utility. It cannot be exploited for profit; you cannot get anything out of it. It is "unproductive," therefore it is regarded as useless. Yet there is more help and healing in silence than in all useful things."*

—Max Picard, Swiss philosopher

There are many ways to make space for silence, and the most common ones are listed as follows. Read through each one and put a check in the box if you could make this a regular part of your life. Being silent is not something that you do once a year. Ideally, you need some quiet time every day. During times of transition or when you need to make important decisions, you may need longer periods of solitude and silence.

❑ **Walks.** Every day, take a walk alone, or silently with another person, for at least 20 minutes. During this walk, focus your attention on the present moment. Try to breathe slowly and deeply. Notice the trees, flowers, the feel of the wind on your skin. What color is the sky? What is the temperature? Use each of your senses to help you stay in the present.

❑ **Journal writing.** There are many ways to keep a journal. Ira Progoff's model, described in his book, *At a Journal Workshop,* is excellent and works for many people. Another useful method is writing three handwritten "morning pages" each day as explained in Julia Cameron's book *The Artist's Way.* For a journal to be most valuable, record the process and flow of your life on a regular if not daily basis. Do not just list the day's events; address the significance of those events, your feelings about them, or your reactions to them. If you do not inquire into the events, you will miss the great potential of journal writing as a means of self-discovery.

❑ **Meditation.** There are many types of meditation, and they all have some elements in common. One method is to spend at least 20 minutes once a day sitting quietly, allowing your mind to grow still. Concentrate on a word (called a mantra) or your breath as a point of focus. As you direct your attention, other thoughts will gradually drop away. In the beginning, you may find it difficult to quiet your mind. With practice you will be able to steady your attention on your point of focus. As you learn to do this, you will notice yourself feeling calmer and more relaxed. Some of the busyness you live with will be replaced with a sense of spaciousness and ease. As you continue in your practice, you will discover more about yourself and become increasingly aligned with your purpose. Meditation is one well-known path to spiritual growth.

❑ **Simplify.** Clean out your closets. Give away some of your "stuff." Do less. Consume less. Look for ways to use fewer products. Take only one bag when you travel. Limit yourself to one vehicle. Ride your bike or use public transportation. Try "slow food" that you cook at home and enjoy rather than "fast food" that you consume while driving or working. Simplicity reduces complexity, which leads to more tranquility and less busyness in your life. If this appeals to you, read Duane Elgin's book, *Voluntary Simplicity: Toward a Way of Life That Is Outwardly Simple and Inwardly Rich.*

❑ **Reflection.** It is easy to lose sight of your life in the midst of living it. Alan Lakein, the author of *How to Get Control of Your Time and Life,* coined the phrase "What's the best use of my time right now?" to help people manage their time. You may want to use this same technique of using a focusing question to help you stay on purpose. Here are some possibilities:

➤ How am I making a difference?

➤ Is what I am doing right now on purpose?

➤ Is this what I really want to do?

➤ Am I following my passion?

You may need a cue to remind yourself to ask one of the focusing questions. One way is with colored adhesive dots that you buy at an office supply store. Place the dots in several places in your office and home where you are likely to see them. Then, whenever you see a dot, stop for 60 seconds and reflect on your life, using one of the above questions or others you create. If you do not like the answers you give yourself, you may need to make some changes.

❑ **Quiet Time.** This is time, usually by yourself, when you eliminate outside distractions. Turn off the radio, the computer, and television; ask family and friends not to disturb you; unplug the phone. In this atmosphere of quiet you can do any satisfying activity—reading, exercising, taking a bath, shooting baskets, watching the sunset, working on a hobby. Quiet time gives you an undistracted opportunity to be with yourself and see what comes up. These are times when your intuition can speak to you.

❑ **Personal Retreats.** In times of transition you may need more solitude than usual. Some transitions you expect, such as marriage and job changes. Others come as a surprise, such as divorce, death, and job loss. When you reach one of life's choice points it can help to have extended quiet time alone. A week or even a night away can be just what you need. Many people find that if the retreat allows them to be outside in nature, it is more healing than if they are confined to an indoor space.

It is very easy to fill your life with activities, to be busy all the time. You may even be praised and admired by others for all you can do. But busyness can never lead you to your purpose. That is an inside job. Solitude balances the busyness with time for yourself. How willing are you to listen to yourself? You cannot know your passion until you do.

Veil #2: What Will Other People Think?

> *"When I follow only the 'oughts,' I may find myself doing work that is ethically laudable, but not mine to do. A vocation that is not mine, no matter how externally valued, does violence to the self—in the precise sense that it violates my identity and integrity on behalf of some abstract norm."*
>
> **–Parker J. Palmer, *The Courage to Teach***

The Tyranny of the Shoulds

You may already know what your purpose is. And you may know how you want to express your purpose to the world. Yet, you may not be fulfilling it. Why not? You may be caught in the tyranny of the *shoulds*.

Shoulds are statements that you hear from others telling you what they think is right or wrong, good or bad for you. Other words that mean the same thing as *should* are *ought, must,* or *have to*. Here are some examples:

"You shouldn't change jobs when you're vested."
"You must stay in your current job until the kids are out of school."
"You ought to take the job that pays the most whether you like it or not."

When someone is important to you it is easy to want to make choices with which they will agree. You may find that you want their approval. Sadly, pleasing others and doing what they think you should do can result in you sacrificing what is right for you.

Take a moment now and ask yourself who the others are in your life that you try to please.

Whom I try to please:

_____

_____

_____

_____

Are you aware that should statements can damage your self-esteem? They lead to feelings of guilt, inadequacy, and blame. People rarely recognize the enormous power that shoulds have to control their behavior and self-perception. More often than not, there is a should between you and your purpose.

There is a difference between consulting with someone to get their opinion and consulting to receive their approval. The latter can paralyze you. If you try to please all the others in your life, you will discover that it is not possible. It is not very fulfilling either.

Could it be that you are trying to please others instead of living on purpose?

ARE YOU PLEASING YOURSELF?

Think back over decisions you made in the past month. Did you make any of them based on what someone else would think, or did you make them to please yourself? How do you feel about each decision?

For example, you might have applied for a promotion because everyone said you should, citing the usual reasons—more money, more prestige. When you actually got the promotion, you may have felt uneasy because you realized that the new job would require you to travel, taking you away from your top value, your family.

Decision #1 and how I felt:

_____

_____

_____

Decision #2 and how I felt:

_____

_____

_____

Decision #3 and how I felt:

_____

_____

_____

Understanding the Three Layers of Shoulds

Making decisions for yourself can get complicated when the various others in your life do not agree with you about what you should *have, do,* or *be.* These are the three layers of shoulds, as described in the examples that follow:

Having **Shoulds—** **You should have:**	• A nice car • A good job • Money in the bank • The latest clothes
Doing **Shoulds—** **You should:**	• Act your age • Listen to the news every day • Keep your desk clean • Check and answer your e-mails every hour
Being **Shoulds—** **You should be:**	• Perfect • Strong • Smart • Successful

Shoulds can limit and constrict your life. But more important, they can kill your spirit. If you should "act your age" (Doing Should), will you ever be able to go to an amusement park and delight in the rides? If you should "be responsible" (Being Should), can you ever take a risk? If you should "be modest" (Being Should), can you accept your gifts and talents?

You may already have let go of the Having Shoulds and perhaps even some of the Doing Shoulds. You might even be tempted to skim over this section, thinking that you have heard all this before. But have you let go of your Being Shoulds? These go so deep that you may not have questioned them. Yet they form the criteria upon which you judge yourself and decide whether or not you are okay.

Despite the pain and limitations that Being Shoulds impose on your life, they are extremely difficult to let go. Why? Because they were forged when you were a child, and they have come to define you. They provide a formula—although an often impossible one—for acceptance. The terror of releasing them is this:

Who are you if you are not your Being Shoulds?

To let go of your Being Shoulds, you need to take responsibility, in the profoundest sense of the word, for yourself.

What are your shoulds? Include Having, Doing, and Being Shoulds, but pay particular attention to Being Shoulds.

My Having Shoulds:

_____

_____

My Doing Shoulds:

_____

_____

My Being Shoulds:

_____

_____

When you let shoulds guide your life, you are living from the outside in rather than from the inside out. In other words, you are giving others control over your life. You are giving others the power to decide whether you think you are okay or not. Then, no matter what you decide, you suffer feelings of guilt, inadequacy, and unhappiness because someone thought you should do something else.

When you live inside out, however, you are able to follow your purpose, rather than someone else's notion of what you should do. Your brothers and sisters may have worked in the family business, but if you feel called to study art, you will be happier and will make a greater contribution if you listen to your calling than if you try to placate the family shoulds.

Fulfilling your purpose requires letting go of shoulds and doing the hard work of knowing yourself. Are you ready to let go of your shoulds and replace them with something that will serve you better?

Removing the Veil: Clarify Your Values

As the shoulds fall away, you will replace them with your personal values. *Values* are beliefs that you choose to guide your life. A key word here is *choose*. Shoulds are absorbed without conscious choice. Values guide you in separating right from wrong in situations. When someone tells you what you should do, you can check his or her should against your values and decide what is right for you.

Not everyone will share your values. Do you judge people when they hold a different point of view? When it comes to values, there is no right or wrong, good or bad; there is only different. As you stop judging yourself, you will stop judging others. When the judging is silenced, you will be able to hear with increasing clarity what it is you really, really want to do.

Write down what you secretly think you would really like to do:

_____

_____

_____

Restating Shoulds to Reflect Your Values

Most of us know what we should do, but it is far more difficult to articulate what we value. Look back over your list of shoulds. Are any of them actually values for you? Write down in the space provided any shoulds that actually reflect values you have. To shift your shoulds to values, you will need to change the way you talk to yourself. Instead of saying, "I should do volunteer work" (which creates guilt), try saying, "I choose to donate time to community service." Other words you can use to replace your shoulds are "I want" and "I prefer."

Should	Value
_____	_____
_____	_____
_____	_____
_____	_____
_____	_____

All the values you have as an individual make up your personal values system. You may have fooled yourself into thinking you behave according to your values. In fact, many people find that it is extremely difficult to do what they believe is right, especially when faced with opposition. For example, you may say you value time with your family, yet you agree to work overtime whenever you are asked, because you "should" be a team player.

To be truly values-led demands integrity and responsibility. Rather than taking a stand for their values, most people slide back to listening to their shoulds. You can guard against this by being clear with yourself about what you do value.

IS YOUR BEHAVIOR IN LINE WITH YOUR VALUES?

Listed below are many values. For each one, rank how important it is to you on a scale of 1 to 10, with 10 being the most important. Then rank your behavior–how well you live your values–using the same scale. If the numbers are more than three points apart, use the third column to write down what action you could take to bring your behavior and your values into alignment.

For example, you may rate your physical health as 10, extremely important to you. But you do not exercise, you smoke, and you eat many high-fat foods. You rate your behavior a 5. In the third column your action plan might read, "Walk 20 minutes three times a week." You can modify your behavior or adjust your values to bring the two into alignment. Use the blank spaces to record any values you hold that are not listed.

Value	Importance	Behavior	Action Step
Achievement	_____	_____	_____
Altruism	_____	_____	_____
Appearance	_____	_____	_____
Arts (music, painting, writing, etc.)	_____	_____	_____
Authority/power	_____	_____	_____
Balance	_____	_____	_____
Beauty	_____	_____	_____
Career/employment	_____	_____	_____
Community	_____	_____	_____
Creativity	_____	_____	_____
Diversity	_____	_____	_____
Emotional health	_____	_____	_____
Environment	_____	_____	_____
Expertise	_____	_____	_____

CONTINUED

52

	Value	Importance	Behavior	Action Step
Family	_____	_____	_____	_____
Freedom	_____	_____	_____	_____
Home	_____	_____	_____	_____
Honesty	_____	_____	_____	_____
Humor	_____	_____	_____	_____
Integrity	_____	_____	_____	_____
Learning	_____	_____	_____	_____
Leisure time	_____	_____	_____	_____
Love	_____	_____	_____	_____
Loyalty	_____	_____	_____	_____
Meaning	_____	_____	_____	_____
Openness	_____	_____	_____	_____
Personal Growth	_____	_____	_____	_____
Physical Health	_____	_____	_____	_____
Privacy/solitude	_____	_____	_____	_____
Recognition	_____	_____	_____	_____
Relationships	_____	_____	_____	_____
Religion	_____	_____	_____	_____
Risk taking	_____	_____	_____	_____
Security	_____	_____	_____	_____
Service	_____	_____	_____	_____
Spirituality	_____	_____	_____	_____
Status	_____	_____	_____	_____
Wisdom	_____	_____	_____	_____
_____	_____	_____	_____	_____
_____	_____	_____	_____	_____

┌─────────────────────────CONTINUED─────────────────────────┐

As you went through the list, did you notice that there were some values to which you assigned a low rank, yet you direct much of your behavior toward those values? That is a clue that shoulds rather than values are controlling your behavior. People often commit their time, energy, and resources to activities that are not congruent with their professed values. For example, you might have ranked service as low, yet you serve on committees in your community and church, and anytime someone calls looking for volunteers you say yes.

Your resources (time, energy, money) are limited. Remember that when you say yes to something, you are saying no to everything else! Clarifying your values helps you make wise choices and escape the tyranny of the shoulds. Saying yes to your passion means saying no to your shoulds.

└──┘

DECIDE WHAT YOU VALUE MOST

Select the five most important values from your list in the preceding exercise and give an example of that value in action during the past week. An example is given for you.

Value: *Honesty*

Example: *When my husband asked if I would like to go out for pizza, I told the truth and said I would rather stay home.*

Value: _____

Example: _____

_____

Value: _____

Example: _____

_____

Value: _____

Example: _____

_____

Value: _____

Example: _____

_____

Value: _____

Example: _____

_____

Did you have difficulty with this exercise? Until you put your values into action, you will not be able to create the life you want. When your behavior is in alignment with your values, you earn integrity.

Replacing Shoulds with Values Statements

Some of your shoulds may not reflect your values at all. In fact, they may be in direct opposition to your values. One of the best ways to let go of these shoulds is to replace them with values statements.

Look back at the list of shoulds you recorded earlier. Some of them were, in fact, values that you converted by changing your language. But the other statements do not represent what you believe. Record these in the left-hand column below. In the right-hand column, write down the value you want to live by. See the examples before you begin. Please notice that you need to decide for yourself which shoulds are not your values. Different people will make different choices.

SHOULD	VALUE
I should make a certain amount of money.	*I want to do meaningful work regardless of what it pays.*
I should spend time on the weekend with my relatives.	*I value solitude and time alone on the weekends.*
I should clean my house and mow my lawn.	*I prefer spending time with my children to doing home maintenance and will hire someone to do these tasks.*
I should buy a new car.	*I prefer spending my money on travel rather than transportation.*
_____	_____
_____	_____
_____	_____
_____	_____
_____	_____

This process has helped you eliminate meaningless shoulds and unnecessary guilt. You have made an active choice about what is important to you and what you believe. Now whenever someone puts a should on you, you can check their should against your values. If there is a match, great! Change the should into a choice and feel the increased sense of personal power. If the should does not align with your values, let it go and refocus on your values.

Resolving Values Conflicts

Sometimes you have two values that seem to compete with each other and you have to decide which of the two is more important. These are usually difficult choices.

Imagine that security is a high value for you and so is service. You volunteer your time to serve the needy in your community while your partner works at a high-paying job allowing you to honor each of your values without conflict. But suppose your partner was laid off and could not find employment. Then what would happen to your values? You might find yourself in conflict between your service and your security values. You would need to choose which value is higher for you. There is no *right* answer. There is only your answer.

The only time to compromise a value is for a higher value. For example, you might value loyalty and truth. What would you do if your boss asked you to do something that you believed was deceitful? If you compromised your values for any reason other than a higher value (for example, because it would be easier), you would lose your self-respect which would lead to the loss of self-esteem.

Sorting Out Your Own Values Conflicts

Values conflicts are painful. They demand that you go deeper into yourself to find your own truth. In the spaces that follow this list of examples, write out the values conflicts you face.

Example: Do I work on the project I brought home from work (achievement) or spend time with my children (family relationships)?

Example: Do I express how I feel (honesty) or remain silent and pretend I agree (sense of community/security)?

Example: Do I fertilize my yard like the other homes where I live (beauty, conformity) or do I refrain from using fertilizer (environment)?

My Values Conflicts:

_____

_____

How will you resolve these dilemmas? The solution to a values conflict is contained in the following paradox:

PARADOX: *The only way out is through.*

Listening to Your Intuition

Another way to avoid the trap of "what will other people think?" is to listen to your intuition. Most people intuitively know what it is they really want to do with their life. As you work through the exercises in this book, you will notice that you have hunches or gut feelings about your purpose. You may hear a quiet voice whispering to you, telling you what your purpose is. This voice is your inner knower, your inner wisdom, your intuition. Will you listen? Or do you discount this way of knowing?

You will not "figure out" your passion; it is not something that the logical mind uncovers. What you are doing when you work through all of the exercises in this book is preparation work. You are preparing yourself to receive the answer to "What is my purpose?" Your answer to the question will come to you through your intuition.

At its most developed level, intuition is your connection to a higher level of consciousness. Jung called this the collective unconscious. Mystics have called it God. The purpose of removing each of the veils is to enable you to better hear your inner knower. Your challenge is not only to listen, but to take action on this knowing. How often have you said after something happened, "I knew it!" but you did not trust what you knew?

Intuition and Outcomes

Think back to times when your intuition spoke to you and you did not listen. What was the outcome? Record three times when you wish you had listened to your intuition.

1. I wish I had listened to my intuition when _____

   because _____

   _____

2. I wish I had listened to my intuition when _____

   because _____

   _____

3. I wish I had listened to my intuition when _____

   because _____

   _____

Letting Go of Blocks to Intuition

Every person is intuitive. Many people, however, do not listen to their intuition. Why didn't you listen to your intuition in the examples you just wrote down? Probably because of distrust, fear, or external listening.

Distrust

To trust your intuition, you need to believe in yourself and trust yourself. If you are not confident in your inner wisdom, you will depend too heavily on logic, analysis, and other cognitive, rational processes. There is nothing wrong with a left-brain approach to situations. By itself, however, it does not give you the complete picture. When you trust your intuition, you get more of the truth. And you get it much faster than when you use your intellect!

Would you listen to a person you did not trust? Probably not. In fact, you would actively tune out the person. The same thing happens when you do not trust your intuition. You drown it out with busyness, thoughts, analysis, preoccupations. It is no surprise that some people claim they have no intuition; they have spent years denying, ignoring, and distrusting it.

It is uncomfortable not to be able to articulate why you know something or how you know it. That is why intuition requires trust. You need to make a leap of faith and trust that this way of knowing is as valid as any other. The more you trust your spouse or loved ones, the more they tell you about themselves and the better you get to know them. The more you trust your intuition, the better you will get to know it too.

Intuition also demands your trust because it comes to you in pieces. You rarely get all the parts at one time. You need to trust that, as you continue down the path, more pieces will be revealed to you. If you like to be in control, this can be very difficult in the beginning.

Fear

Some people try to silence their intuition out of fear. They are afraid of what their intuition might say and that they might need to make a change if they listened to their intuition. Once you are aware of what needs to be done, it is hard to respect yourself and maintain high self-esteem if you do not take action. Are you afraid to act on what you know?

You may realize intuitively that your passion is to create beauty through your love of plants and your talents in landscaping. If you currently work as an accountant, you are in an uncomfortable situation. To be true to yourself, you need to take some action on your intuitive knowing, no matter how small. Your integrity is at stake if you do not.

It is so much easier, so much safer, to say to yourself, "I know I'm not happy in my work, but I just don't know what I want to do." Then you can safely study the situation. You get ready to know rather than risk knowing.

Be honest with yourself now. What do you know, but hesitate to admit to yourself, because of the action you would need to take?

_____

_____

What scares you about taking action?

_____

_____

External Listening

How often have you discounted your intuition because it did not agree with what someone else thought? Do you put more credibility in your friends' opinions than in what you intuit? Do you try to meet other people's expectations instead of listening and following your inner knower? Do you relinquish your truth for someone else's truth?

Fulfilling your purpose means that you are willing to take personal responsibility for your life. You accept the challenge to live a courageous life from the inside out. You become the expert on your life, not someone else.

When you let others dictate the decisions you make about your life, you put them in control. When you go along with others, you betray your own inner wisdom. Each betrayal is a silencing of your intuition. Eventually you only listen externally. But internal listening is essential if you want to hear your intuition.

When did you let someone talk you out of trusting your intuition?

_____

_____

How did it turn out?

_____

_____

Amplifying Your Intuition

After you let go of any blocks to intuition, you will be in a better position to tune in to your intuition. Follow these four steps to "turn up the volume" and amplify your intuition.

Step 1: Preparation

Your intuition puts pieces together into a whole, but it needs the pieces to do this. The more information, learning, and experience you gather, the more your intuition can draw from to create an intuitive "flash."

Step 2: Incubation

You have undoubtedly had the experience of trying to solve a problem, but try as hard as you might, no answer would come forth. Later, while you were mind-lessly taking a shower or driving somewhere, the answer magically appeared as if from nowhere.

The answer needed time to incubate. After you prepare your mind by giving it everything you know about the problem, you need to give your intuition time to work on it. Assume an attitude of openness to receive the answer your intuition offers. You may work all of the exercises in this book and still not feel clear about your purpose. Let it incubate. Eventually you will get an...

Step 3: Aha!

This is the moment of awareness. The answer comes to you. Sometimes it seems obvious, but other times you may feel uncertain, hesitating to trust what you sense.

Intuition speaks to each person in its own way. Some people report that they experience their intuition as a feeling about something. Others describe a gut reaction. Some see an image or picture of what they need to do or they have a dream. Still others hear a message. You need to acquaint yourself with how your inner knower communicates with you. This is important because you can confuse wishes, hopes, and fears with intuition. Each of these is different.

Wishing and hoping are both thoughts. Intuition is not a thought; it is an instant, immediate knowing. There is no rational process.

Think about times when you know that your intuition spoke to you. How did it communicate with you? Be as specific as possible.

_____

_____

Step 4: Verification

Test your intuition against reality. Try out the idea. See if it works. You may need to collect more information before you act on your inner wisdom. For example, you might get an intuitive flash to move to another part of the country. Before you sell your home and pack your bags, do some research.

Veil #3: I'm Not _____ Enough

> *Everyone has his own specific vocation or mission in life to carry out a concrete assignment which demands fulfillment. Therein he cannot be replaced, nor can his life be repeated. Thus, everyone's task is as unique as is his specific opportunity to implement it.*"

—**Victor Frankl, *Man's Search for Meaning***

66

Rethinking Your Perceived Shortcomings

Are you beginning to realize that by removing each veil, you are peeling off the ways you have stopped yourself from knowing or fulfilling your purpose? This third veil addresses how inadequate we can sometimes feel when we try to fulfill what we are called to do. We can feel we aren't "good" enough or "smart" enough or "educated" enough.

In what ways do you feel you are "not enough"? Write down all the reasons that come to mind.

I'm not _____

_____enough.

More often than not, you feel as if you are not enough when in fact you are. Remember the characters in *The Wizard of Oz?* Tin Man, Scarecrow, and Lion were all seeking something they did not believe they had. A funny thing happened when they got to Oz and met the wizard. They each discovered they already had what they were seeking. They just had not acknowledged it. Is it possible that you too have all that you need?

Acknowledging When You Were "Enough"

In the spaces provided, list three situations in which you were indeed "enough." It might help to think of times when you believe that you made a difference in some way.

I was "enough" when:

_____

_____

I was "enough" when:

_____

_____

I was "enough" when:

_____

_____

Now look back at how you filled in the previous blanks "I'm not_____enough." In any of the three situations you just listed, did you have "enough" of that *something* you thought you lacked?

Avoiding the Comparison Trap

Sometimes you may feel fine about yourself—until you start comparing yourself to someone else. The comparison trap is very seductive because sometimes you "win." Sometimes you do come out smarter or more talented or better in some way. Unfortunately, other times you lose and feel inadequate, or less than, the other person.

Look again at how you are not enough and ask, "compared to whom?"

I'm not _____ enough compared to _____.

I'm not _____ enough compared to _____.

I'm not _____ enough compared to _____.

I'm not _____ enough compared to _____.

What did you discover? Are you making comparisons? Such comparisons are counterproductive because they do not take into account your unique talents, skills, values, and purpose.

The sooner you stop comparing yourself to others, the sooner you will be on your way to knowing and living your own passion.

Removing the Veil: Raising Your Self-Esteem

Self-esteem is how you feel about yourself. You either like yourself or you do not. If you do not like yourself, it will be very difficult for you to trust yourself enough to listen to your intuition, which will tell you what your passion is. Even if you do listen to yourself, if you have low self-esteem, you probably will not risk acting on your knowing. You will not feel you are "worth it."

Like a three-legged stool, high self-esteem is supported by three things. First, you need a feeling of "I can," or a sense of competence. You explored this in Veil#1 when you identified your talents and skills. Second, you need self-respect. Veil #2 described how shoulds can erode your self-respect, and how values enhance your self-respect. The third leg of self-esteem is self-worth. Self-worth comes from knowing your uniqueness. You will have an opportunity to explore your uniqueness in this part of the book.

SELF-ESTEEM INVENTORY

Here is a list of statements that people with high self-esteem tend to mark true. Read through each statement and mark it either *True* or *False*.

T   F

☐   ☐   1. I can admit a mistake.

☐   ☐   2. I can reach out to people I do not know.

☐   ☐   3. I maintain my values even when others do not approve of them.

☐   ☐   4. I can accept a compliment without feeling uncomfortable.

☐   ☐   5. I can be myself around other people.

☐   ☐   6. I accept myself with all my faults and weaknesses.

☐   ☐   7. I can tell you my strengths.

☐   ☐   8. I can feel joy for someone else's achievements.

☐   ☐   9. I do not compare myself with others.

☐   ☐   10. I have peace of mind.

☐   ☐   11. I believe I am unique.

☐   ☐   12. I can let my playful inner child out without worrying about what others will think.

☐   ☐   13. I accept differences in others without judging them.

☐   ☐   14. I affirm myself and others.

☐   ☐   15. I openly express my love for others.

☐   ☐   16. I love myself.

☐   ☐   17. I accept all of my feelings.

☐   ☐   18. I enjoy my own company; I am comfortable being alone.

The more *Trues* you have, the higher your self-esteem. Fewer than 13 *Trues* indicates your self-esteem needs a boost. Keep working through the exercises in this part to help you feel more positively about yourself.

Analyzing Your Self-Talk

You talk to yourself all day. In fact, you have been talking to yourself as you read this book. During these internal conversations, you may be planning, worrying, rehearsing, or remembering. As you engage in these thoughts, you might also be judging yourself.

For example, if you are *planning,* you may think, "I don't know how to do this, I'll never figure it out." Or perhaps you are *worrying* with thoughts such as "I bet I don't get the promotion because I'm not as experienced as the other candidates." If you are *remembering,* you might think, "Why did I say that—it was such a stupid thing to say."

It is these judgmental thoughts that cause feelings of low self-esteem. What you say to yourself affects how you feel about yourself. For the next hour, pay attention to your self-talk. Jot down what you say to yourself. Then carefully review it. As Dorothy Briggs, author of *Celebrate Yourself,* asks, "Are you in the building business, or the wrecking business?"

Putting Your Self-Talk on Paper

Keeping a self-talk log is similar to keeping a time log or a food journal. It lets you see in writing what you are saying to yourself. Once your self-talk is on paper, you can analyze it for shoulds, judgments, and other negative thoughts. Reading what you have written can bring a painful awareness that you are damaging your own self-esteem with the language you use. Yet, until you know what you are doing, it is not possible to change. On the lines below, write down some of the things you are saying to yourself right now.

_____

_____

_____

After you become aware of how you judge yourself, you can move to the next step, which is to say "Stop!" when you catch yourself starting to judge. With some practice, you will become very good at blowing the whistle on yourself. Then you can begin replacing the judgment with positive self-talk.

Giving Yourself Daily Acknowledgments

How often have you gone to bed at night rehashing in your mind the mistakes you made, the errors in judgment, the words spoken that were better left unsaid? When you do this, you erode your self-esteem. To increase your self-esteem, try giving yourself daily acknowledgments instead.

A daily acknowledgment consists of taking a few minutes before you go to bed to recount to yourself 10 things you did that you feel good about. These do not need to be grand accomplishments. The quality of your life is measured by the little things. Reflect on the day for all the positive things you said or did. If you fall asleep remembering the things you feel good about, you will awaken feeling good about yourself.

Keeping a Daily Acknowledgment Journal

The following page may be photocopied for your personal daily acknowledgment journal. Take a moment now to write your list for today. You can add to it tonight if you like. At the end of each week, review your daily acknowledgments for the entire week—all 70 items! As your list grows, your self-esteem will grow.

The following example of one person's daily acknowledgments will help you see the kinds of things you might include.

1. I got out of bed when the alarm went off.

2. I took time to pet the cat before I left for work.

3. I kissed my partner good-bye and said "I love you" with feeling.

4. I let three people merge into my lane while I was on the freeway driving to the office.

5. I returned two phone calls without procrastinating.

6. I said "thank you" when the mail carrier dropped off my mail.

7. I gave someone my full attention when I listened to him.

8. I turned the TV off when the show I wanted to watch was over.

9. I ate an apple for dessert instead of cake.

10. I hung up my clothes before I went to bed.

MY DAILY ACKNOWLEDGMENTS

1. _____
2. _____
3. _____
4. _____
5. _____
6. _____
7. _____
8. _____
9. _____
10. _____

73

Finding Your Purpose

Keeping a Gratitude Journal

Some people find that the best way for them to quiet the judging mind is to create a list of things for which they are grateful. You might want to keep a gratitude journal instead of, or in addition to, your daily acknowledgments. Simply take time at the end of the day to list at least five things for which you are grateful. Here is an example:

Gratitude Journal

1. I am grateful for my friendship with Maria.

2. I am grateful for a sunny day.

3. I am grateful for the great service at the restaurant today.

4. I am grateful to have a job I enjoy.

5. I am grateful to hear the birds sing.

Begin your own gratitude journal using the lines below.

1. _____

2. _____

3. _____

4. _____

5. _____

Replacing Negative Self-Talk with Affirmations

As you have learned in this part, building your self-esteem involves changing your negative self-talk in several steps. The first step is to become aware of what you say to yourself with the self-talk log and to practice interrupting negative thoughts with the word *stop.* The second step is to write out your daily acknowledgments or keep a gratitude journal. The final step is constructing positive statements, or *affirmations,* that eventually will replace your negative self-talk.

With an affirmation, you affirm, in the present, something you want to create in your life in the future. Remember, you are today who you thought you were yesterday! In other words, if you have been telling yourself you will never find the right job, you are probably working right now at something that you do not find fulfilling.

If you continue to think the same way, you will continue to get the same outcomes. You can change this pattern, however, if you change your thinking. Start today to affirm that you have meaningful work, and you will create that outcome for yourself in the future. Henry Ford was right when he said, "Whether you think you can or think you can't, you are right."

Rules for Effective Affirmations

Affirmations are statements you make to yourself that describe the life you want. They can be about anything. You might start with affirmations related to your self-esteem. The more you like yourself, the more you will trust yourself and the more likely you are to share your gifts with the world. For any affirmation to be most effective, keep in mind the following rules:

Rule #1: State affirmations in the present tense.

Your behavior tends to mirror what you believe. When you state something to yourself as if it were true today, your behavior will come into alignment with the belief more quickly than if you state it as being true in the future. For example, if you are looking for a new job, you will not get as positive a result saying "I will find a good job" as if you were to affirm "I have the job I desire."

Rule #2: State affirmations positively.

Your mind can work more effectively with affirmations that express what you want than statements that express what you do not want. For example, "I accept myself" is more powerful than "I don't criticize myself."

Rule #3: Use affirmations every day.

As you know, you talk to yourself all day long. Your affirmations need a chance to be heard amid all the negative self-talk. Say them frequently, but say them at least every morning and every evening. If you say your affirmations as you fall asleep at night, you will be programming your subconscious mind when you are relaxed and more susceptible to suggestion.

Rule #4: Empower your affirmations with feeling.

When you say your affirmations to yourself, evoke as much feeling as you can. This is like supercharging your affirmation. You remember things that you feel. Recall a favorite movie or book. You probably remember it because it touched you on a feeling level. Express your affirmation with feeling and you will create it faster!

Write Your Own Affirmations

Using the following sample affirmations as a starting point, write your own. Start with no more than two or three. As you bring the first few into reality, you can add others.

1. I now accept myself.

2. Every day, in every way, I am growing more and more healthy.

3. I let go of negative thoughts.

4. I am a loving person.

5. I love and respect all of my natural abilities.

Now write your own:

1._____

2._____

3._____

Check what you have written against the four rules for affirmations. If you need to make any changes to what you wrote, do so.

As with daily acknowledgments and gratitude, you will begin to notice a difference after about one month of using affirmations. You will be pleased with the results.

I am coming to realize that my purpose is:

_____

_____

_____

_____

Discovering Your Uniqueness

As you gain clarity about your purpose, you will discover that it has a synergistic effect on your self-esteem. Once you realize you are here for a purpose that only you can fulfill, you find there is no need to compare yourself with anyone else. Everyone has a unique passion. Each person will fulfill his or her purpose using his or her own set of talents and skills. How and where you use your gifts to fulfill your purpose will depend upon your personal life experiences. No one else on the planet is exactly like you.

As you raise your self-esteem and feel better about yourself, you will come to know yourself better and to know what makes you unique. This knowledge will help you fulfill your personal purpose. You will bring to bear all of your life experiences—good and bad—all of your talents, all of your skills, and all of your hopes to make an impact on the world.

Reflecting on Your Skills, Talents, and Experiences

To remove Veil #1, you were asked to list your talents and skills. Very often people with low self-esteem have difficulty identifying their talents. They find it hard to believe that they are unique. Was it hard for you to list your talents? Here is another opportunity.

Take some time to reflect on the questions that follow. Use what you have discovered so far about your skills, talents, and values to help you. If you do not have an answer now, listen to your intuition for a sense of the answer. Let yourself live in the questions over time and the answers will emerge. Your willingness to ponder each question is as important as the answer.

1. What skills and talents make me unique?

   _____

   _____

2. How have I used my uniqueness to affect my world?

   _____

   _____

3. How does my personal set of life experiences enable me to make a difference in the world?

   _____

   _____

4. When have I made a difference?

_____

_____

5. How did I do it?

_____

_____

6. Is that a clue to my uniqueness?

_____

_____

7. When have I felt most alive, energized, and present to the unfolding of my life?

_____

_____

8. Deep in my heart, why do I believe I am here?

_____

_____

PARADOX: *The question is the answer.*

P A R T 5

Veil #4: Fear

"Not only does every individual have a prophetic vocation, but every individual has prophetic vocations. As times change, and we change, and our responsibilities in a changing culture change, we are called to let go sometimes of past prophetic calls and to immerse ourselves in new ones."

—Matthew Fox, *Original Blessing*

Understanding the Veil of Fear

With the other three veils removed, you now reach the fourth reason that you may have hesitated to follow your heart. Are you afraid? There are two kinds of fear associated with pursuing your passion.

First, you may be afraid to know what your passion is. Why? Because once you know, you are confronted with the responsibility to take action to follow your passion. You can allow yourself to be passive only as long as you "don't know" what you want to do. Most people want to be in control of their lives, yet few want to accept the responsibility that goes along with it, and they use fear to avoid knowing. Could this be true for you? Are you afraid to know the truth?

The second fear occurs once you know what your passion is. This is the fear, as mentioned above, of taking a specific action toward fulfilling your purpose. For example, you might need to go back to school. And perhaps you are afraid of this.

Categories of Fear

The fear that holds you back from knowing and fulfilling your purpose is not physical fear. It is psychological fear. In other words, it is not an outside threat, but an internal threat. There are five major categories of psychological fear:

> **Failure:** Being laughed at, not doing it right, not knowing how to do it, making a mistake, not being capable.

> **Success:** Being overrun with the success, losing friends because of it, overworking or becoming a workaholic, gaining notoriety, being consumed, having too much responsibility.

> **I will get hurt (physically):** The stress of it will make me sick; it might kick up my ulcer; I will have a panic attack; I will not be able to breathe.

> **I will get hurt (emotionally/psychologically):** They will not like me, I will be rejected, I will be excluded, I will be embarrassed, I will not be able to cope, I will make a fool of myself, my mate will leave me.

> **The unknown:** I do not know what will happen, I do not know what to expect, I will not be able to cope with what happens, I will not know what to do.

WHAT DO YOU FEAR?

What fears are holding you back from living on purpose?

My fears of failure:

_____

_____

_____

My fears of success:

_____

_____

_____

My fears of getting hurt physically:

_____

_____

_____

My fears of being hurt emotionally:

_____

_____

_____

My fears of the unknown:

_____

_____

_____

085

Interpreting Fear as a Step Toward Growth

Fear occurs when you live in the future instead of the present—when you worry about what *might* happen. Look at the fears you listed in the preceding exercise. Aren't they each related to something that *might* happen? They are not present-moment realities.

Yet to get to the future, we often need to let go of the present. Fear is an emotion that often accompanies letting go. It is a sign that you are growing. The more attached you are to what you have, who you are, what you believe today, the more fear you will experience. Here are some examples:

➤ If you are invested in believing that you are smart, bright, and quick to understand, then you will experience fear at the invitation to grow into areas in which you have little knowledge. You will need to let go of being knowledgeable to take on the role of learner.

➤ If you are attached to your view of yourself as in control, you will be afraid to let go and be spontaneous. Being relaxed and without a plan will scare you.

➤ If you like seeing yourself as independent, it will be scary to let go of that self-image and ask for help.

➤ If you are attached to your good-paying job, you will be afraid to let go—to try work that promises more fulfillment.

Growth is a continuing process of going beyond. It is not rigid; it is flexible. It changes. To find and fulfill your purpose, you will be called to let go of where you are and go beyond. What must you let go of to move closer to your passion? What scares you about letting go?

When will you feel fear? Usually at moments when you are about to stretch yourself toward new growth. Fear is a sign that you are entering a personal frontier. It is associated with uncertainty as well as a sense of adventure. It involves risk. Not feeling fear before you do something is an indication that the task at hand is not big enough for you. Think of fear as a reassuring signal that you are on the right course.

Finding Your Purpose

Recognizing Your Sense of Fear

Fear is an uncomfortable feeling. Consequently, people often try to hide their fear or to overcome it. But, like any other emotion, fear does not respond well to these tactics. It works better to understand and befriend the fear. How do you do this? You begin by recognizing fear as soon as it arrives. To do this, recall one of the fears that stops you from doing what you really want to do. Once you have the feeling clearly in mind, "five-sense" it using these questions:

Where Do You Feel the Fear?

For example, for some people fear lives in their stomachs. When they get the sensation of butterflies in their stomachs, they know it is present. For some, it lives in their legs. The expression *knees knocking* describes their fear. Now describe where your fear lives.

_____

_____

What Does Your Fear Look Like?

Imagine drawing a picture of your fear. How big is it? What color? What shape? Is it abstract? Now draw that picture of your fear in the space provided.

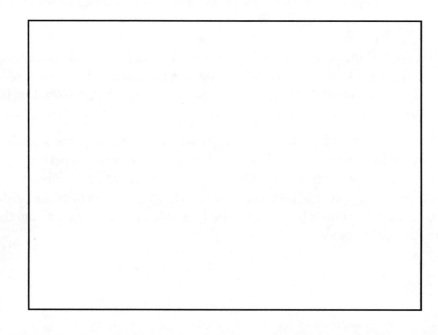

What Does Your Fear Say?

List the words that your fear uses when it speaks to you. This is especially important because it is often what fear says to you that prevents you from taking action toward what you really want. Once you learn what fear typically says to you, you can learn to talk back! Some people's fears issue warnings such as "You will be sorry! Don't do it! You can't! You will fail."

My fear says:

_____

_____

How Does Your Fear Taste?

Be as descriptive as you can. Rather than saying "bad," try to be more precise. For example, "My fear tastes as bitter as a 50-mile-an-hour wind whipping my face on a subzero winter morning."

My fear tastes like:

_____

_____

How Does Your Fear Smell?

Again, be as descriptive as you can. For example, "The smell of my fear is noxious and clinging, like smoke clinging to fabric long after a fire is over."

My fear smells like:

_____

_____

By completing these questions, you may discover that your fear is not as awful as you first thought it was. On the other hand, if it is truly a monster, now that you can see it clearly, you will be able to cope with it more effectively. The unknown is always more frightening that the known. You have just made your fear known to yourself!

HOW DO YOU RESPOND TO FEAR?

Do you try to eliminate fear? Overcome it? Deny it? Avoid it? Worship it? Befriend it? Research it? Ignore it? Talk about it? Take action? Below, record three times in your life when you felt afraid, then describe how you coped with the fear.

Situation #1

Fear:_____

_____

How I Coped: _____

_____

Situation #2

Fear:_____

_____

How I Coped: _____

_____

Situation #3

Fear:_____

_____

How I Coped: _____

_____

Befriending Your Fears

Fear is not your enemy! If you befriend fear, it can be an asset to you. A tremendous amount of energy is associated with fear. You have undoubtedly heard stories of people who showed superhuman strength when they were faced with fear. In research studies, students who felt some fear about taking a test did better than students who felt no fear. Your goal is not to eliminate fear, but to harness it.

Let fear be a catalyst for your growth!

Fear can be transforming or it can be constricting. You decide which one it will be for you. If it is to be transforming, you need to identify what you are afraid of and then look behind it for the growth that is trying to break through. Focus your attention on your goal and let go of where you are.

> *What the caterpillar calls the end of the world, the master calls a butterfly."*
>
> —**Richard Bach**, *Illusions*

To support this transformation you need to focus on what you want—your goal—rather than your fear. Then the goal, rather than your fear, will become your motivator. Use the energy the fear produces to take specific action steps that will bring you closer to your goal.

PARADOX: *To eliminate fear, embrace it.*

List your fears about following your passion in the left-hand column of the chart below. In the center column, write down what you want—your goal. In the third column, write the action steps you could take to achieve your goal. An example is completed to help you get started.

FEAR	GOAL	ACTION
I will not get promoted	*To become a supervisor*	*Identify a mentor and ask for guidance on how to prepare to be a supervisor*
_____	_____	_____
_____	_____	_____
_____	_____	_____

For many people fear leads to being stuck, to settling for what is rather than risking what is possible. You cannot find your purpose, much less fulfill it, without befriending your fears. And as you may have surmised from reading this page, befriending those fears and achieving your goals requires taking a certain amount of risk.

ARE YOU COMFORTABLE TAKING RISKS?

Complete the following questionnaire to find out your comfort level with taking risks. For each question answer *yes* or *no*.

Y or **N**

1. I don't take as many risks as others might because I know my limits.

2. I seek others' approval before I take a risk.

3. I believe it is better to be safe than sorry.

4. I need to feel in control in most situations.

5. If some action scares me, I stop doing it.

6. I take a risk only if there's nothing to lose.

7. I feel uncomfortable with uncertainty.

8. I prefer to do things the way I have always done them.

9. I hate to make a mistake or be wrong.

10. I think things change too quickly.

11. I research any risk before I go forward with it.

12. I feel uneasy around people who take lots of risks.

13. I have trouble acting on what I believe.

14. I change my mind easily if other people disagree with me.

15. I can't remember the last time I took a risk.

16. I sometimes wish I had taken a risk in a situation.

17. The first thing I consider before taking a risk is what could go wrong.

18. I have difficulty asserting myself.

The more *yes* answers you have, the less of a risk taker you are. If you have more than nine *yes* answers, pay special attention to the next section to help you to increase your risk-taking behavior.

Removing the Veil: Taking Risks

"*Courage is not the absence of fear; rather, it is the ability to take action in the face of fear."*

—Nancy Anderson, ***Work with Passion***

As with each of the other three veils that may be keeping you from finding your purpose, there is a way to remove the veil of fear—and that is by developing the courage to take risks. Risk taking is a skill that can be learned. And like any other skill, you get better at it with practice.

Levels of Risk Takers

Your answers to the questionnaire in the preceding exercise will give you an idea of your starting point in learning the skill of risk taking. Are you a nonrisk taker, a calculated risk taker, or an impulsive risk taker? Let's look at each level in more detail.

Nonrisk Takers

These people like to play it safe in all situations. If you fall into this category, you answered the Risk Questionnaire with at least 12 *yes* answers. Nonrisk takers are unlikely to know their passion because to know it would demand that they take some action. Not knowing is much safer. If they do become aware of their passion, they complain about why they cannot fulfill it. Complaining is safer than being responsible for their life. Chances are that if you are a nonrisk taker you feel powerless over your life.

Calculated Risk Takers

These people take planned risks. They consider the possible benefits as well as the probable consequences of an action. They weigh their alternatives before they act. They see mistakes as a learning opportunity, not a failure. They want to grow and stretch themselves. Calculated risk takers recognize that there are no guarantees and plan accordingly. Even as they go forward with a risk they have a Plan B in mind in the event things do not go as they hope. They are not afraid to acknowledge when they make a mistake. Because of their careful planning, they often do not perceive their actions as risks.

Impulsive Risk Takers

These people love the thrill of a risk! They like to live dangerously. They do not consider the downside of a risk. They wear blinders and see only the outcome they want. Often the important people in their life feel uneasy with many of their actions. For impulsive risk takers, the sense of danger is what gives them satisfaction, not achieving a specific outcome. If you answered *no* to all the questions in the risk questionnaire, you may be an impulsive risk taker.

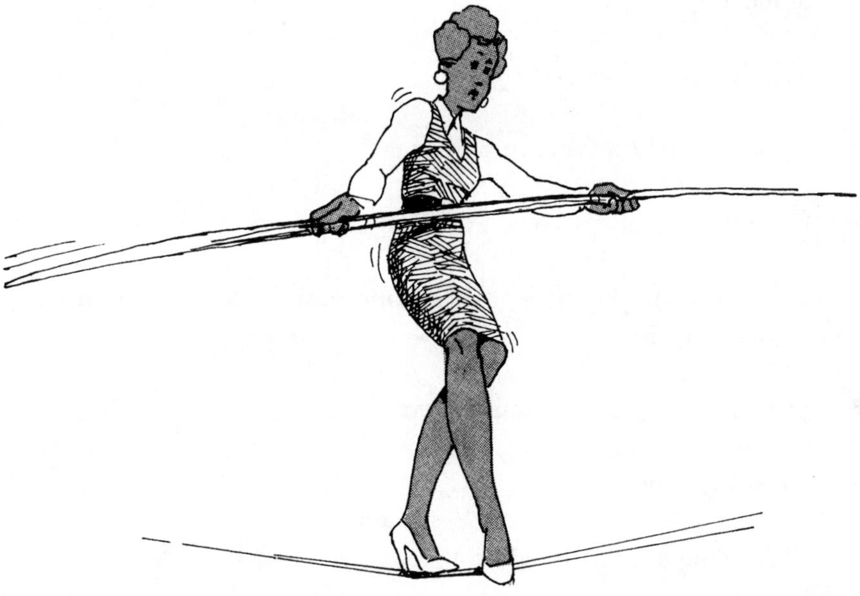

Getting Started with Smaller Risks

Before you take the big risks in life, you need to experience success with smaller risks. To increase your risk-taking behavior, follow the advice of Bill McGrane II, founder of the McGrane Self-Esteem Institute, who said, "Stretch yourself to be uncomfortable every day." Let's look at ways you might do this.

You could:

➤ Drive a new route to work

➤ Be the first to say hello to people you pass on the street

➤ Smile at strangers

➤ Tell the truth sooner

➤ Apologize when you are wrong

➤ Compliment people when they do something you like

➤ Call someone you do not know but would like to meet, and suggest getting together

➤ Say, "I love you," to someone you love

➤ Do something silly

➤ Risk being embarrassed

➤ Ask what a word means when someone uses an expression you do not understand

➤ Do nothing for half an hour

➤ Speak out at a meeting

➤ Express how you feel

➤ Disagree with someone

Using this list as a starting point, write down in the spaces below at least five ways you could stretch yourself to be "uncomfortable" in the coming week. Then do it! As you do, you will find yourself able to take bigger and bigger risks.

As Dame Iris Murdoch, the British novelist, wrote, "At crucial moments of choice, most of the business of choosing is already over." If you do not learn to be a risk taker today, you will not be able to take a risk when you are faced with a big opportunity. Your moment will pass because you were not ready.

Risks I will take:

1. _____

2. _____

3. _____

4. _____

5. _____

Taking Steps to Improve Your Risk Taking

There is a systematic process that will help you feel more comfortable taking risks. If you practice these 10 steps, you will discover that you can take bigger risks, feel less fear, and fulfill your purpose.

Step 1:   Start small. As your comfort level increases, so will the size of your risks.

Step 2:   Collect as much information as possible about the potential risk.

Step 3:   Consult with other people. Note that this is different from seeking their approval.

Step 4:   Ask yourself, "What is the best possible outcome?"

Step 5:   Ask yourself, "What is the worst possible outcome?"

Step 6:   Ask yourself, "How likely is the worst possible outcome?"

Step 7:   Ask yourself, "If the worst possible outcome occurred, what would I do?" If you do not have an answer for this question, this may not be a risk you want to take.

Step 8:   Ask yourself, "What is the probable outcome of not taking the risk?" You may have forgotten that continuing to do what you are doing can be very risky. Your present course is not safer simply because it is familiar. For example, you may be considering changing jobs and think a new position is risky. But if you suffer from headaches or another physical ailment in your current work, you may be risking your health if you do not make a change.

Step 9:   Evaluate the outcomes of the risks you have taken. Did they turn out as you expected? If not, why not? What have you learned for the next time?

Step 10: Celebrate your successes. When you take a calculated risk and you achieve the outcomes you wanted, give yourself credit for taking a risk. Gradually you will come to see yourself as a risk taker.

PART 6

Veil #5: The

Seduction of More

> "More money, more tokens of success—there will always be people for whom those are adequate goals, but those people are no longer setting the tone for all of us. There is a new sort of more at hand: more appreciation of good things beyond the marketplace, more insistence on fairness, more attention to purpose, more determination truly to choose a life, and not a lifestyle, for oneself."
>
> —Laurence Shames, *The Hunger for More*

Rethinking the Quest for "More"

The mantra in Western (and particularly American) culture toward the end of the 20th century and into the 21st has been "more, more, more." Even spiritual seekers were being seduced by it, collecting spiritual experiences and practices like any other commodity. Then came the dot-com collapse and the tragedy of September 11, 2001, which became wake-up calls inviting many people to rethink their values and what is really important.

You have lost your purpose when you think that what you do is less important than how much you get paid for doing it. You are off purpose when choosing meaningful work is less important than choosing work that pays well. When "more" is the driver, enjoying life takes a back seat to having a lifestyle.

Your purpose is never about making money. Your net worth does not determine your self-worth. Materialism, consumption, and having *things* can never take the place of the inner work that is necessary for a life of meaning.

Where does the cultural bias for "more" show up in your life?

1. _____

_____

_____

2. _____

_____

_____

3. _____

_____

_____

The Downside of Getting the Things You Desire

Many people think that having things will make them happy. But if you are "lucky" enough to attain the things you desire, get ready for two rude awakenings.

> ➤ **Having does not make you happy.** The advertisers promised that when you had a particular car or lived in a prestigious neighborhood or dressed a certain way you would be happy. They lied. Happiness is an inside job. It comes from being who you are, fulfilling your purpose, and living your values. Things are empty sources for meaning. Desire only leads to more desire.
>
> What have you wanted that, once you got it, did not give you the joy, satisfaction, or happiness that you expected?
>
> 1. _____
>   _____
> 2. _____
>   _____
> 3. _____
>   _____

> ➤ **Things are not guaranteed.** You can lose them. Thousands of people lost their jobs during the dot-com collapse and the Enron scandal of the early 2000s. When the jobs went, so did the lifestyles they were supporting.
>
> Furthermore, life itself is not guaranteed. We will all lose loved ones—expectedly or unexpectedly. Life is fragile; it passes in a moment. Are you living your life on purpose? Or have you traded a purposeful life for a lifestyle that can change in a moment?

The more disconnected and alienated you are from your *self,* your inner purpose, the more likely you are to look outside yourself, to material things, for meaning. As Matthew Fox wrote in *Original Blessing,* "It is not letting go of things that is important, but the letting go of attitudes toward things."

Examining the "Have, Do, Be" Formula for Happiness

In *To Have or to Be?* Eric Fromm described a misconception that many people hold as a "formula" for happiness. You might too. He said people spend their lives trying to:

Have enough (money, resources, things) so they can...

Do what they want (in relation to work, how they spend their time), because then they can...

Be happy.

Unfortunately, most people get stuck at the first step. They never *have* enough. Perhaps you have said to yourself, "When I have the car paid off, I'm going to make a change." Then when you pay off the car, you say, "After I get the kids through school, then I'm going to make a change." One day you reach the end of your life and realize you have never done what you wanted to do with your life.

Reversing the Cycle

Fromm says that to have a satisfying life you need to invert the formula. First, you need to:

> *Be* who you are. Know your strengths, your values, your purpose. This self-awareness will lead you to...

> *Do* what you love. This doing will be the contribution of your unique gifts. Because you are giving yourself away, you will be rewarded, and you will...

> *Have* what you need. Of course, there are no guarantees you will have everything you want! As Dick Leider writes in *The Power of Purpose,* "There are two ways to be rich. One is to have more; the other is to want less." To reach the stage of having requires patience. While you wait, you need to define yourself by who you are, not what you have.

How do you turn the having/doing/being cycle around? You stop making *having*—money or things—the goal. You stop measuring success by your bank account and possessions. You get your priorities in order and follow your heart, guided by your values.

Removing the Veil: Shifting to *Being*

The having mode is certainly seductive. But by definition, having is possessing and it can disappear as easily as it came. The being mode is not so transient. In this mode you are centered, authentic, connected to your spiritual self. You have your personal power to assist you in creating and fulfilling your passion. If you can comfortably be yourself—without living from your "shoulds"—your need for outside approval disappears.

From the centered place of being, your vision of who you are can express itself. You will be drawn to your passion. In the having mode, you feel driven. It is no coincidence that you hear about being *market-driven* or even *values-driven*. These concepts come out of the having mode. The language of purpose, on the other hand, is values-*led* or customer-*led*. What feels better to you—being driven or being led?

The Influence of Inspiration

Think back about times when you have felt inspired—times when you were drawn to a person or idea. Recall situations in which you thought to yourself, "I'd like to make that kind of impact." When you felt inspired you may have noticed that you reacted physically with shivers up your spine or tears of awe. Describe three situations when you felt inspired.

1. _____

_____

2. _____

_____

3. _____

_____

As you reflect on these situations, were you pulled to take any action? Your passion can be an inspiration to you if you let it be.

Deepening Your Understanding of *Being*

It is difficult to understand what it means to *be*. We spend more of our time doing or having. The following list provides a deeper look at *being qualities*. As you study the list, put a check mark (✔) beside the ones you have experienced. Put an X in the box beside the qualities you would like to develop.

✔ or X

☐ **Ability to be with.** Can you be with yourself quietly, alone? If you cannot be with yourself, you probably do not accept yourself. And if you cannot be with yourself, how can you be with anyone else? You will want to change them or control them instead. Most important, if you cannot be with yourself, you will find it extremely difficult to express your passion.

☐ **Present to the moment.** *Being* occurs only in the now, this moment. To be demands that you stop living in either the past or the future. When you are in the moment, you are open to life as it unfolds. This present awareness allows you to see and take advantage of opportunities as they present themselves. When you are able to stay in the now you will notice that you feel less fear and experience less stress.

☐ **Awareness.** Do you say "I have a problem," or do you say "I feel troubled?" The second phrase is from a state of being. You are aware of how you feel. You are aware of yourself in relation to the rest of the world. Rather than possessing your experience, you are aware of your experience. When you think in terms of having or possessing, the next logical step is to control, conquer, or overcome. Today our relationship with the environment is a classic example of the negative effects of this way of relating to the world.

☐ **Responsibility.** You are responsible to your purpose, to bring it into reality. This is not a responsibility *for,* but a responsibility *to.* Your ability to respond comes directly from your state of being. To be yourself requires action; it is not a passive state.

☐ **The observing self.** Ironically, as you increase your awareness, stay more present to the moment, and develop the other qualities of being, you will discover that you have a level of consciousness that observes all of this. Even as you read and complete the exercises in this workbook, there is a part of you that can observe you.

- ❏ **Practice.** A practice is something you do regularly, often daily, to awaken and deepen some part of yourself. Examples of practices include keeping a journal, meditating, playing an instrument, or practicing a martial art. As George Leonard wrote in *Mastery,* "You practice diligently, but you practice primarily *for the sake of the practice itself*" (emphasis in the original).

- ❏ **Spontaneity.** When you are in the moment, being with life as it unfolds, you will discover that there is less need to have everything planned. You can live on the edge of uncertainty where you do not know what you will think or feel next. This is a juicy place to live.

- ❏ **Kairos time.** The Greeks had two words for time. Kronos was used when referring to clock time. That is the kind of time that flies by or drags on. Kairos time is when time itself becomes invisible; it seems to stop. You do not have any sense of time passing because you are completely engaged in being.

- ❏ **Authenticity.** When you are in the being state, people experience you as "real." You risk being vulnerable with what you feel and think. You express who you are. In moments of authentic contact with another person, all the veils are gone.

- ❏ **Intuition.** You will have greater access to your intuition when you are in a state of being than when you are in the having or doing mode. Intuition will guide you toward authentic action in the moment.

PARADOX: *What is to give light must endure burning.*—Victor Frankl

---

Reaching a Conclusion About Your Purpose

Now that you have looked through the five veils, your purpose may be very clear. If it is not yet completely clear, you undoubtedly have a better idea of what it is, and you know which veils you need to remove so that your purpose does become clear. Be patient with yourself.

Do not let the veil of fear prevent you from declaring a mighty purpose. Your purpose may be to feed the world. It may be that your purpose is to ensure justice. Your purpose could be to awaken spiritually. Purpose is at the center of your being and it radiates from you. When your purpose is compelling and uniquely yours, it guides you to a fulfilling and satisfying life.

With a purpose that is big enough to hold you throughout your life, there is room for you to manifest it in any number of ways during your lifetime. If your purpose is to feed the world, you could be a farmer, a fund-raiser, a writer, a social activist—or all of these at different points in your life. In your 20s or 30s you may be thinking of your purpose as a career. Your purpose can encompass many careers, and it is bigger than any of them.

Remember that your purpose will flow through every domain of your life. Refer to page 14 where the domains are listed to be sure that your purpose can be lived out in every one of the eight areas, even if you are not yet prepared to do that.

State Your Purpose, Mission, and Vision

In the box that follows, write your statement of purpose as you now understand it. It will probably be a brief, succinct, compelling statement. Then you can add a second line that describes how you will do it. This is your mission. It will describe the talents and skills you possess to fulfill your purpose. And finally, you can add a brief statement that describes the outcome if you fulfill your purpose. This is your vision. Here are some examples.

Purpose: *My purpose is to teach.*

Mission: *I will use my love of words and my gift for establishing rapport with others to fulfill my purpose.*

Vision: *A literate world.*

Purpose: *My purpose is to serve.*

Mission: *I will use my talents for listening and leading.*

Vision: *Workplaces that uplift the human spirit.*

Purpose: *My purpose is to be a force for awakening.*

Mission: *I will do this using my writing and speaking talents.*

Vision: *Everyone in the world will be enlightened.*

Purpose: *My purpose is to be a voice for diversity.*

Mission: *I will use my communication and facilitation skills to ensure that all the voices are heard.*

Vision: *A world in which everyone is equally valued.*

My purpose is:_____

My mission is:_____

_____

My vision is: _____

_____

Final Word

Finding your purpose is an inner journey. Only you can answer life's most demanding questions. Yet you have a companion—this book. Let these exercises guide you to deeper levels of awareness. The question of your purpose will not be answered once and for all. It will evolve as you move through your life. Like the process described in this book, the answer will emerge as you create it.

This journey you are on is literally your life. Savor it!

PARADOX: *This solitary work we cannot do alone.*

Additional Reading

Buckingham, Marcus, and Donald Clifton. *Now, Discover Your Strengths*. NY: The Free Press, 2001.

Cameron, Julia. *The Artist's Way*. NY: Tarcher/Putnam, 1992.

Fox, Matthew. *The Reinvention of Work*. NY: HarperCollins, 1995.

Frankl, Victor. *Man's Search for Meaning*. Boston: Beacon Press, 2000.

Hanh, Thich Nhat. *The Miracle of Mindfulness*. Boston: Beacon Press, 1975.

Leonard, George. *Mastery*. NY: Plume, 1991.

Levoy, Greg. *Callings: Finding and Following An Authentic Life*. NY: Three Rivers Press, 1997.

Palladino, Connie. *Developing Self-Esteem*. Crisp Series, 1994.

Kindler, Herb. *Risk Taking, Revised Edition*. Crisp Series, 1999.

Tolle, Eckhart. *The Power of Now*. Novato, CA: New World Library, 1999.

Whyte, David. *Crossing the Unknown Sea: Work As a Pilgrimage of Identity*. NY: Riverhead Books, 2001.

NOTES

110

NOTES

Also Available

Books•Videos•Computer-Based Training Products

If you enjoyed this book, we have great news for you. There are over 200 books available in the *Crisp Fifty-Minute™ Series*. For more information visit us online at www.axzopress.com

Subject Areas Include:

Management

Human Resources

Communication Skills

Personal Development

Sales/Marketing

Finance

Coaching and Mentoring

Customer Service/Quality

Small Business and Entrepreneurship

Training

Life Planning

Writing

OUR SENSE OF THE ORDER
IN THINGS IS A LIVELY, AND
VERY SIMPLE SUBSET OF
THE ACTUAL ORDERING
OF THINGS.